GLASS HARVEST

GLASS HARVEST

Amie Whittemore

Autumn House Press

Pittsburgh

This project was supported by the Pennsylvania Council on the Arts, a state agency, through its regional arts funding partnership, Pennsylvania Partners in the Arts (PPA). State government funding comes through an annual appropriation by Pennsylvania's General Assembly. PPA is administered in Allegheny County by Greater Pittsburgh Arts Council.

Cover photograph: Laura McPhee, *Judy Tracking Radio-Collared Wolves From Her Yard, Summer Range, H-Hook Ranch, Custer County, Idaho, 2004,* from *River of No Return.*
Book & cover design: Joel W. Coggins

ISBN: 978-1-938769-16-0
Library of Congress Control Number: 2016938925

for my family

&

for Tim

CONTENTS

III. *Inventing a Seashell*

GLASS HARVEST

"You must go down the long stairway
Into the dark coal sack of the sky;
O love, O longing, O world that was before."

Ruth Stone, from "End of Summer...1969"

Aphorisms

If you can admit your own narrowness,
you're onto persimmon and cardamom.

If you dust off your brave pants, you'll manage
mudslides, samba, dodge and weave.

The smallest voice is the truest;
wear those ears that turn like planets.

If you give him a turnip,
and he turns to sand, begin again:

the tax you pay for loving is grief—
my therapist said so, and once you accept

a therapist's wisdom, you're halfway
somewhere. Goats are sympathy machines

unlike squirrels, toads, mirrors, livers,
harpoons. Doors—

they multiply every time you walk through one.
When you're doing something,

you're doing something. Lift a hand,
mouth, or heart. Draw the shades.

I. DREAM OF THE ARK

Dream of the Ark

My brothers will not name their sons Hiram, though I see them—
bird-chested boys with floppy ears and big noses climbing trees

and throwing rocks through windows of abandoned garages,
their shouts springing kernels from their cobs.

But when my brothers and I speak of our future
children, it's like children reconstructing the lives of dinosaurs.

We argue, and those shirtless barefoot rascal boys
are whisked back into their husks. I dream my womb

is an ark, filled not with children, not pairs of animals, but leaf blight,
broken spinning wheels, severed hands warped with arthritis.

~

Morning. Watching the half-frozen river collect geese,
I know I'm a fool for whatever's gone away.

I tell my husband my dream of the ark, another of raising canaries
in a basement, their bodies yellow ornaments in trees prospering

without sunlight, their rattled leaves sparking like aluminum.
And while I interpret these visions as signs we'll never grow

blueberries, gather eggs from hens, he looks at me
like I'm speaking Dutch. He says too often I extrapolate

an entire imaginary alphabet from a single letter.
In other words, *relax*. Outside, his shovel slings snowdrifts.

~

But I know my brothers will not name their sons Hiram,
and I will have no daughter named Kathryn,

though she often appears, smoking a joint on the beach,
her new skull tattoo laughing on her shoulder.

She hates when I call her lily-pad.
She flings curse words at the sky like empty beer cans.

Mile-long hair, voice like moss-coated stone, I imagine
her into more and more beauty, while also fashioning

her a weak heart. I warn her the future is a skinned animal
stalking us all. I tell her the swan's neck is a noose.

Winter trees braid the white sky; my husband shakes snow
from his boots and comes inside.

~

We drink tea. I remind him today is the shortest day.
But what I mean is, I want to unbutton the future

and find a breathing lung. I mean, if we indulge in a dream
of new Hirams and Kathryns, new Edwins and Whitts,

if we kissed open their eyes, inhaled their birthy scent,
would the other dream, of keeping the farm, of replanting orchards,

of raising goats, vanish? Neither dream is trustworthy.

My desire is like a child's wish for her toy doll
to mend its broken leg. My husband would argue you can't mend

what isn't broken. My brothers would suggest I'm in love
with an idea that doesn't exist. They're probably right.

But I hear the doll weep. I feel her broken leg like it is my own.

The Unknotting

Sour cherries splatter the burnt lawn;
a black dog wears its clover necklace.

Rabbit caught, a fluttering heart in my palms.
Wagons piling with gold beads of soybeans,

sweet pop of pods chaffing the yard.
My grandmother like a queen in all this, distant,

as if always on the swing hung from the oak.
Charmer—even the dog would hold her hand

in its mouth. Who wouldn't want to please her?
Woman who tucked her dresses into overalls

to haul corn with my grandfather,
who knew grosbeak, goldfinch, junco,

whose call pulled swans to her like water.
How to answer when she asked, standing

beside her old photograph, if she was beautiful?
Sunset-colored hair, eyes two pools singing

about the sky. I'd go back now and ask—
nothing. Whatever lies between fact

and invention is too slim to matter.
Just let me draw near them—small self

and Grandmother, braiding clover—a bee
fretting their hair, seeking blossom.

Hayloft

Nowhere is there
light sloshing up
and down your arms
like it did that time
you climbed the ladder
to the hayloft.
Nubbin of cat purr,
scurry of small unseen;
what will you do here,
small one, limber
and brittle as these
aging floorboards?
No one is watching—
not even the slatted,
dust-freckled sunlight.
Slim column of empty
boxes for a spine,
I'd like to roll you
over the edge,
fork the unforked past.
How you tremble,
thinking this forbidden
climb is bravery.
I don't want to hear
anything pretty boom
in your chest. I won't
supply dragonfly wings,
shoe squeak, centipede feet.
Darling self,
no one cares
how we sculpt ourselves
from rags and dashing.

First Visitation

for my great-grandmother, Kathryn

When she arrives, quiet as a thimble,
I want to throw a chair at her—instead, I weep.
Kathryn scribbles out a family tree, but she

might as well be a squid, this ghost unbraiding
my hair, rubbing my shoulders. Her voice
rakes all the leaves. Harvests me. That boy.

I try to show her. How it was like he
threw a teacup on the floor and I ate
every piece. How it was like long grass forever.

She makes my womb a swallow's nest. I break
it in half. She replaces my feet with eagle talons.
I cut them off. She turns my heart into a bucket—

this one I'll take. But I empty it out.
Water swims around us and we are both
ghosts. My bedroom washes away. Then

the house. Outside, fireflies gather us
into their baskets of light and carry us
first to the trees, then to their mouths.

Ten Walls

First: November's gray shroud flush
against sky, my father and I
quiet over cereal, radio reporting
the Berlin Wall falling. I pictured
a second wall, barbwire ratcheting
free of its posts, rolled up
in a giant porcupine, our cattle hesitant
to hoof the gap. The third: photograph
torn in half, taped back together.
A decade later, the fourth emerged
when I told my lover I wanted
to cheat on her; she kept me,
and I knew how prairie felt
once mowed, fenced, made lawn.
Frost is right, *something there is*
that doesn't love a wall
but then I knew something in me did.
For the fifth, I built a brick border
around yarrow, gay feather, sedum.
That border showed me the Wall
as a multiplication of bricks,
wan math dividing blood
from vessel, hand from wrist.
No wonder that winter sledgehammers
slung over shoulders of *Mauerspechte*
sounded like woodlarks cleaving song from stone.
The sixth is my inability to tell this right.
The seventh takes me back to that
November when none of my classmates
discussed the Wall, though it weighed on me,
a child, who knew two things for certain:
one, she was ugly.
Two, she was trapped behind an impenetrable wall

only someone irrefutably handsome could demolish.
And if the eighth is realizing she'd have to be dynamite,
the ninth is the stickiness of that story—
that someone *will* rescue you from the tenth wall,
as if the self could finally be
your body tugged free from an ill-fitting dress.

Blackberry Season

We toss blackberries at each other's mouths
as if they are tiny grenades—

their stains swelling like bruises.
We ignore the handful of blue eggs held aloft

in my hand, fingers a nest of tangled thread.
Thin pain in my wrist. The tilt of your chin

makes me think you mean red velvet cake
when your beer and berry breath leans

in for a kiss. Not once have you asked
to touch the eggs, though they are smooth

as the word *yes*, heavy as *no*. Blackberry seeds
turn our tongues to sandpaper and my skirt

thrown across the floor looks like a lake
where a child has drowned. You set to work,

turning our bodies into jam. I can't look at you,
strange man, without thinking of the woman I left,

those small pumpkins that were her breasts.
Migratory as the blackberry, I landed in Portland,

forgetful of home, though my legs
wrap, root-like, around your waist—

I blame the incessant rain for these eggs in my hand.
I spin them like Chinese medicine balls.

That's the faint chime you hear in the morning
after the fuss and sweat, after we slept

like patients recovering from surgery. Awake,
you say my name like you're practicing scales.

I won't ask you back. You were a costume
to wear, so I could (for a night) forget the eggs

nested in my hand, deposited by some malicious
Midwestern bird. A trick. Blue as robin song.

Velleity

That longed-for ghost, my unborn daughter, looked
like the quivery flicker of fish across a pond's skin.

If I held her, I'd see that other land where the dead
and unborn live in lake-colored clothes, hair messy

with marigolds. I won't say what I promised her
to make her follow me to Illinois, my grandparents'

empty house. Where grief roosted, we unclipped its wings.
Opened every window. Snapped all the rugs.

Before she daydreamed under a sky stitched
in swallowtails; now she likes geese wintering

on the hoary river. She smells like old novels.
Her hand in mine, pressure on a bruise.

∼

For a while, I called her viridian, mayapple, life raft,
and her babbling matured into a willow's green straps.

For a while, she never aged, never asked for her absent
imaginary father. For a while our lives were happy scenes

pasted to a garden mirror. But, like all children, she found
contrary interests and, afternoons, bounced

a tennis ball against the shed door. Locked for hours
in her bedroom, she'd emerge, maps of the world drawn

on her arms, hair no longer a toddler's gosling feathers.
Before long her feet, then her heart, would turn her

like the moon, one face always away from me. I told her to go
back to that unlife, the seasonless world where you belong.

I warned her it only gets sadder—spoiled girl,
she slapped me. She lifted her shirt and showed me

a torso tattooed in Latin, every species of dying
frog, every white-nosed bat. Smog frothy on her chest.

Whether we fought or stewed in silence, does it matter?
It was her skin now—she could hate it. Love it, too.

The Quarry

That stone crown
flooded turquoise.

Up from the hidden
spring, mermaids

plumed. They wheel
in this unlikely

aquarium, feathers
of milk and rubies.

One summer
they dragged

a boy down
to their watery beds.

His father tossed
poisoned minnows

into that gravel mouth—
summering geese ate them.

Their dark bodies
sank like sorrow.

Trapped, the mermaids
clack the boy's bones

against the quarry walls,
faces pinched like silk.

Last Visit

Try to remember the last rain—
dry gauge swabbed in a torn cocoon.
Do a little skit of happiness
for the grandparents, all daffodil smiles
and foxtail tickle. Homesickness
like a collapsed lung. Like a collapsed house,
you, the single jar of pickled beets to survive—
please, let's sit in a sunroom.

They look out the window, talking
about the cardinal. Always bopping its head
against the window the way you do against this poem.
Are you sick of Grandfather's cane? Of the soiled spot
on the armchair where his head slowly disappeared,
like a drift of bees rolling out and out?

Go ahead, wave a wand over their eyes,
steal the stale bread, cast it in the river like a spell.
That cardinal's winking at you now;
you're on the same side of the glass.
Poor dandy of a bird—finicky apple with wings—
give it what it wants. Tie a knot. Hope it sings.

Two Widows

We installed another widow
to keep Grandma company.

She came with a parakeet,
or maybe her husband returned,

for it fell from the sky after his funeral
and strutted only when she entered the room.

The widows played backgammon, tried to agree on food.
Still, on Christmas day, Grandma pleaded—

I can't go back to that house.

But our hearts are more balance beams than see-saws.
We opened the door, kissed her cheek, not saying much.

What were we thinking? What had we done
but hang bent mirrors before both their faces?

I too would have collapsed on the couch
on a Thursday in March, my shoes slipped off

like toy boats cast free. I too would have left
my body like a hammock, swinging slow.

Yard Catalog

cattle tongues

brother's voice

skunk

black dog

tulip the size of

my hand

snowbreak

dried well

lawn mower

oil buckets

dove in silo

dove in dust

withered lilacs

daffodils

the dead leaves

the windows

my hands inside

black dog

darkbloom

that papery

hornets

ruined blue flowers

clear stone

chicory

black dog

my hand

among crocuses

barn door

dead skunk

that droning throne

dark shed

dove in gravel

bathing my hands

cattle spine

yellow in

yellow in

walnut leaf

owllight

bleeding paw

snow caught

cold faucet

those echoes

Second Visitation

A galaxy of firefly corpses scattered on my bedroom floor;

Kathryn, Great-grandmother, the sun they circle.

Kathryn, the novel's unread chapters keeping me awake.

~

I don't know how she sees me—
                              a tick tapping her skull

or what I'd like to be
                              for her, milkweed seed,

sack of shorn hair she hands me: my wings.

But within, her cut strands churn,
                              a nest of garter snakes;

cinnamon-stained tails, mouths white as hail.

~

When I speak,
                              she turns to the window.

Her spiky scalp glows in the moonlight.

Beneath the blue drape of her nightgown, another snake,
                              this one dead—

a scar across her stomach.

Tell me, I urge her. But she's silent as a folded map.

~

Maybe she wants to know
                    what it's been like

these decades since earth ate her bones.

Maybe she's looking for the lantern idling in my chest.

                        ~

Milkweed stains the air
                    like wine stains lips.

What sounds she makes crawl over me
                        like sleep. Like sleep

I can't translate. Her nightgown stops

at her ankles. Yes, they look like mine, also like

                        dials to uncrackable safes,

her life unassailable, the numbers that would open,

                    spilled pearls.

                        ~

The dead bugs alight
                from the floor.

It's cinematic the way they dress her

                  in a gown that blinks off and on

the way the mind does

                or the heart—

~

Gone like a star whose light still
                              undresses me, she

won't return. Her gaze

splits me like a swallow's nest.

My shorn hair, scattered on the floor,
                                        no closer to a map.

Drowning the Marigold

If every diary is a prayer, leave them clasped
as palms. If all I say is split

like a coin—half true, half foul—
know that when I drowned the marigold

my brother planted for my mother,
it was spite, not accident.

Know that I wanted the bees to live forever
in our barn slats, that I still wake wanting

to watch my father and uncle, home from farming,
eat sandwiches on rye. I want to keep the hate

I felt for that grassy flavor, which I love now,
as I do so many tastes, not so much acquired

as surrendered to. I'd trade red wine
and bitter beers, darkest chocolate, for those

childhoods I keep polished as coins in the satchel
of my chest: dew climbing my feet as I

walk to the sapling I planted and weep,
so fretful of its survival I'm tempted to pull

it from earth, its dirt-thick roots
the matted hair on a newborn's skull.

The Clarinet

I wake up thinking of clarinets.
Saddest of instruments, sexless and lovely.
Their notes, perched mid-air,
those gold plums I ate last night.
They tasted like Grandfather's death.
I saw him again, planting seeds by hand.
My father and I watched like crows.

We're still crows eight years later. Strangers
mock our feathers, our cagey memories,
the way we watch and watch the empty field.
We won't transmute. Though for a second,
that clarinet remade me human.
Its golden fruit heavy in my mouth,
I was flightless again, after the molt.

The Ancestors

find me in the pasture, each carrying a jar of honey
and an apricot stone, each wearing a skewed version
of my face, the flesh misaligned to bone. They never speak—

no, they do, but by pointing. One to the carriage
of a deer's ribs hung from a branch. One to nettles'
fuchsia blooms. One to my closed mouth.

They never offer the fruit pits, honey jars.
Their dated names rise in my mind like waves—
Pelatiah, Frances, Hiram, Stone—not ghosts, exactly.

Nearer to vision, pollen sprung from blooms.
They point to the tuft of fox fur snagged on barbwire,
horseshoe rusting on a fencepost. We approach the gate

past which I become a different person, past which
(we know the rules) they'll never walk. The women
in long dresses wet at the hems. The men in thick jackets.

They sway like a chorus. But what humming brims,
swells from the gate—a caul of flies. The air cools.
The ancestors fidget as if waiting for a dance to begin.

I'll never get it right—what to say and when
to leave. I point at the crow perched on the corncrib,
cows lowing from the barn, fog uncurling like ferns.

~

II. PERPETUAL MEADOW

~

Charlottesville, 7 a.m.

after Elizabeth Bishop

A stranger kissed me at a party last night.
First with her eyes. White arrow of her chest
inside the white envelope of her shirt—snow on snow.

Winter lives under a pigeon's wing.
Branches crack beneath their glass harvest.
Juncos punctuate the bleached yard, chip silence.

My husband sleeps, his body stretched like a tightrope
diagonally across the bed. Sometimes, the wet flutes
in his throat sound like a raccoon is trapped there.

The woman's lips—soft and tough as a fox's padded foot.
It arrives now, bloodstain on a gray hood.
It tests the earth like morning.

In Oaxaca

Women sold grasshoppers dusted in cayenne and salt,
a swarm's worth, though they were piled, *muertos*, in barrels.
My shabby Spanish limped along: *Quiero, quiero.*
Donde está la biblioteca? No puedo ayudar.

Our friends' wedding paraded down *las calles,*
mujeres in bright embroidery, baskets of dahlias
balanced on their heads, giant puppets, five-piece band,
rain jeweling the bride's forehead—

This city where the lid came off.
This city where we found the trap door.

My husband and I opened secret jars; they lavished us
with cardamom, salt rim, seashells, wing-shed dust—
Lo siento, lo siento, I chimed in the streets,
apologizing for the lids, the jars themselves,

their pickled squid and cumin-coated swarms.
Más vino, más vino, por favor. Ven a mi.
Fuck this unsealed present, *mi cuchara, mi amor, mi cerca de.*
Let's never hear that bird singing like a hinge.

The Hope Boat

Slim craft
we climb

into again
we feel

like autumn
leaves swallowing

shedding sunlight
craft wobbles

beneath
our weight

like water
we throw again

our trust into this
waxed husk

half by row
half by wind

your heart cupped
in my hands

mine a stoneless
peach in yours

The Wife Show

Stirrups. Much. Pantyhose
and paper cuffs. Isn't far
toward. I kissed him all.
There and below. I know
I like those things now.
But always dishes, always
stays and scruff. Keep.
The audience applauding.
Keep. The lightflood
and your bows, keep
those shoulders that long
neck. Turned. Like a slip.
Always tomorrow and its
chain of tomorrows. No,
leaping, no. Keep. Much.
Garters and ruffs. Back
turned and a moment off.
This isn't. Much. Keep.
Coming off. Nowhere
was a stage less a stage
than when it was.

Crush

My mind's oatmeal again,
heart a trapeze, daylight

so pulchritudinous, I'd lie
in grass till sunset, pinned

to lips, torsos, tongues,
thighs (all yours and mine),

rose petals clamping my throat,
the end of this sentence not resulting

in your body pressed against me,
so I'll abandon it for—

I can't walk around like this.
This isn't real life—I hate saying that.

Upon marriage, I thought such seasons
of melt and flourish would vanish.

Yet it's spring all the time,
peony-headed and prone to fall apart.

Look what you've done to me,
half-stranger, half-pearl.

The White Doe

Cantering white rag, hooves like enamel.
Only her tongue dark as soot. Only her tongue
a dark lake culling the forest leaf by leaf.
Rambler. Witch. Surrender's charm.

Asleep among her cousins, whose tawny hides
turn them to dead leaves, she's milkbloom.
Winters envy her, summers pity.
Ghost. Angular cloud. Tumult of light.

Smelling of violets, she tugs me, thread by thread.
Somehow, her blank canvas is always painted—
no binoculars would help. No hoof-tripped trap.
White vine. Leap. Albatross breast.

Compass Plant

"It is easy now to predict the future. For a few years my
Silphium will try in vain to rise above the mowing machine,
and then it will die. With it will die the prairie epoch."
                              —*Aldo Leopold*, Sand County Almanac

Silphium, whose leaves, those bristled arrowheads
slim to slip noonshine, forgive me for calling you
"squat sunflower" all those years I watched
your globes dismantle in the wind-sacked ditches.

I want that ditch feeling again, alone with you,
other misnamed relics. Envious of the giraffe leg
that is your root. After envy expires, your milk
will stain me. Don't worry, I'll forget.

Perpetual Meadow

It's alchemy, the conditions required to persist—

   (establish a greeting ritual, hold hands when you argue)

altitude, salt sprays, rain or its absence. Every meadow slips its frock

   (if you dream of folding a tent, if you hear twig snap)

when balance wobbles, climate shifts, or shade encroaches.

   (reserve a date night, fall asleep holding hands)

Sunning kingsnakes and nesting harriers fret—

   (if his weathers shift, if your joys no longer match)

elk grow claws, transform to bobcats. Quail thin into jays.

   (conjure a good night ritual, hold hands like tourniquets)

Sorrel and bee balm skip town or form a feast

   (if your heart wilts, if his grows antlers)

for bellicose oaks. Without watch, without care, forest migrates:

   (unpeel your bark, unclench his fists)

meadow wanes. Fault the grazing animal gone extinct.

   (if every point is moot, every ritual a disguise)

Fault what can't be repaired: too little heat, not enough salt—

   (fashion a faultless heart, make a harvest of air)

Last Waltz

Mimosa's peach blush drift, pulse
of fireflies, my damp hair on your skin—

lavender dried and twisted in the closet.
Fistfuls of weeds withering on the lawn.

I close and open like a blind.
Finch and trowel, air molasses thick.

Red clover and milkweed crowd
the dead raccoon's flattened mask.

Beneath seed-shake of katydid
and locust, waltz with me, lost plum,

before my hands fill with pumpkin seeds.
Before autumn wraps you in its frayed cape,

let the dove lay its oboed notes down.
Wisteria drapes its piecemeal shade

across our arms. I take your hand,
which still smells of soil and work.

My throat gathers ash.
The whip-poor-will pines for its name.

Another Beach Poem

The ocean is not brave.
Though it mimics desire—
ebb, throb, repeat—
it craves nothing.
A mastiff digs a giant hole,
shoveling after the shell
its owner's thrown.
Ravish me, we say to our lovers.
How boring that grows.
As usual, I pretend something:
The dog gutting a deer,
my body a lightning whelk.
As usual, I envy all
that's not human.

Widow Variations

for Gail

Maybe she heard her husband's
cancer like a bird trapped in a wall.

Maybe she buried a new emptiness
nightly—vase, wine glass, his belt,

his hat. His socks.

Maybe she's closed those three years
of his vanishing like a shop,

key always in her pocket,
door impossible to unlock.

～

First I thought to call it doubled:
both lost their minds

before losing each other,
Ruth and John, Great Aunt and Uncle.

But perhaps their loss is squared,
mind fleeing like autumn leaves—

a ravishing bright and fragmented.

John would surface, calling Ruth
when she was present but gone;

again, when she was gone but present
in the narrowing cave of his mind.

Maybe *cave* is too gloomy.
If metaphor is all we have,

let it divine echoing mind
not as night, subtraction of stars,

but saturation. Names displaced by color—
ochre, vermillion, turquoise, pearl—

Ruth, a fiery opal.

~

I can't make this up: Gail, after digging
three wells and finding only thirst,

after beading and unbeading three ropes
of freshwater pearls three times,

buried her husband on my wedding day.
I can't make this up: a sundog looped

the sun. Nor this: beneath my vows,
as if from the bottom of a well,

I pushed my hand against her heart.
To clench the bruise, the very bruise

I promised myself to. And I wept.
And our guests called it sweet.

But my aunt, months later, said no:
You saw what you were getting yourself into.

~

Gail slips into lingerie's
                weathered net so it
may gather him
                as sweat pooling
behind her knees
                between her breasts
cupped in her ears
                her tongue—
her body a net
                heft to shore
its store of delicate fish
                mimicking
a dreaming brain
                thrashing
unable not to be alive.

~

Ruth and John are gone.
My grandmother manages what's left—

their paintings, their rings, their clothes.
For her, this stings of forecast—

She imagines my grandfather as snowmelt,
a drift of swans receding.

~

A new bruise billows in Gail's chest.
On her wrist, a tattoo of a swallow,

ring in its beak, and in her mouth
always one grain of sand.

I slipped that net early,
closed up my marriage like a shop.

The key in my hand is cold.
I don't know what it locks, unlocks.

Dear Mockingbird,

collect raindrops on tin roofs, luggage zipping,
wind-rattled windows, take wine glasses

I'll never use, smash them in your jukebox heart.
Nab caterwaul of equitable division of assets.

Lend me melodies that join key jingle to foghorn.
Play for me the sound of mates unmating—

I pretend it's the sound of books closing.
But we both know it's forgetting.

Promiseless bird, tireless collagist, gather toilet flush,
cat pissing in its box, pencil snap, paper crumple,

sound of no whiskey over ice, his hand not moving
the record needle, no favorite song—take the dot dot dot

of this my typing, uninterrupted by his jokes, his—

624 White Street, Key West

Hand in hand, we stand before her house.
Bishop recalls lizards dusting her windowsills,
the man, a parakeet latched to his shoulder,
who visited the Civil War cemetery every December.
We name him Sam and invent three children,
a dead wife; we give him a schooner.

It's night and the green light above the door
casts bright confetti onto the palm, the sapodilla—
I ask if she wants to see the flat screen TV,
tinseled and pink Christmas tree, woman
toweling her hair in an upstairs window.

I want a metaphor here; I want Bishop to provide it.
Instead I ask if I can call her Elizabeth
though I hope, eventually, we'll turn to pet names—
we're only pretending to hold hands.
At least I am. Her arms folded across her chest,
I can't tell if she's sad the gutters sag, the paint chips.

A white cat watches us.
Part of me thinks part of her is glad—
the art of losing, etcetera, etcetera.
Perhaps its demise makes this house
more hers than ever—another secret she won't proffer.

Opposite of Blue

Maybe it's the garnet ring he's taken back,
husband, the flavor of thyme and honey,
the papery sound of retreating seabirds.

I'll never tell him iguanas lay eggs
beneath the graves in Key West,
that those eggs are the color of a secret

and the sound of rooster crow.
Nor of the kapok with its vast knees
like a wild gown. Grief that tastes

of salt and snow, you're the opposite
of blue. Your ways are silk.
Your voice a toad's, uncorking the night.

This Empty Bowl

I thought I could sit down in darkness.
I thought the soul an empty echelon,

a blank harvest. I consulted the ledger
of old lovers, that flimsy accounting—

one a telephone cord buried
like placenta. One a dripping faucet

sparking in the night. Another, torn
blouse posing as lampshade.

Echo chamber, resilient flesh,
I meant to say this bowl shines

for you. This darkness, a loan.
My body, remembering its debts,

longs for your bright ship, sings,
turn here. Stay, sweet prow.

III. INVENTING A SEASHELL

Spell for the End of Grief

No incantations, no rosemary and statice,
no keening women in grim dresses.
No cauldrons, no candles, no hickory wands.
No honey and chocolate, no sticky buns.
No peonies and carnations, no handkerchiefs.
No dark and lusty liaisons.

Only you and me to see it out.
Sweet self, let me wash your toes,
brush your hair, let me rock you gently.
Together we'll change the sheets
and I'll pull you to me, little spoon.
You be the marrow; I'll be the bone.

To My Future Granddaughter

It's sweet you want to know me
the way sunlight discerns a leaf,
but this plan of yours to pretend
I'm nearly dead (you get your morbidity
from your father's side, you know)—
just so I can say whatever
the hell I want? Well, here goes.
I was in love with a woman
whom, in my head, I called with all sincerity,
the most beautiful girl in the world.
We kissed twice. We parted ways.
I thought it would happen again.
It didn't. Or hasn't.
So, do with that what you will—no,
hold on. Okay, look.
Whatever you're about to do, stop.
Listen to the acorn in your chest.
If you do right by it,
a tree will grow inside you.
Even if the sanest person—
your mother, for instance, I know
how she can be—disagrees.
You were born a white girl
in the first world to a family whom—
well, you know—we took you to the beach.
Your mother bakes a mean lasagna
and your father talks to crows.
You've been given a lucky start
so, as someone once said to me,
suck it up, buttercup.
No one, not even your mother
with her impeccable sock drawer,
truly gives a flying fuck.

You're afraid, that's all.
It's stupid we're built this way—
I know I'm an old lady with a nose ring,
but once I was an idiot tornado,
drilling into earth, treating myself like disaster.
Blustery, full of despairing wind,
it took me ages to stop and slowly—
so slowly! You think walking me
across the grocery parking lot is slow?
Slower than that, my nugget, slower than that.
I kissed the man who would have been
your grandfather goodbye—
not for a good reason,
just because I wanted to,
and none of this tornado business
could make me feel otherwise.
Oh, that we could be different
creatures, my love. That you and I
could be swallowtails or toads,
humpback whales or harpsichords.
Sweet-pea, I'm tired.
Fetch me a glass of water.
Tell me what it is you want to hear.

Rattlesnake Master

I knew its blooms, like ellipsis among coneflowers, wouldn't cure me.
Though I collected those green-white doorknobs,
though it nodded enthusiastically about light.

If I sucked its taproot after a bite, I'd still unclot
and cool like those tuberculosis patients
who once sought the "healing air" of Mammoth Cave.
Paraffin, spotty coughs, soft footsteps punctuating the dark—

beneath every prairie is another prairie.
Parsed of color, roots like nesting vipers,
it threads through fungi a pale network,
whose velvet and dew crumbles in my fingers.

Loam whets the air. A borer moth clamps
a Rattlesnake Master's stalk, shooting alerts
through root-webs; poison rises in spines.
I imagine a braid through the dark—

those TB patients holding hands, last becoming first,
as one wades toward (they are certain) that mouth
                             where daylight lolls like a tongue.

Memory Palace

by clover
forest of pearls
soft basket
marvelous
rain kept
in your voice
singing
wasn't it your
wasn't it
and sequence
through clover
stinging nettle
sunset's rusted mailbox
hoe over shoulder
but oh those
before our names

remember sunset
all loose in a pocket
of your name
and often
kept keeping
that flapping pocket
the wherewithal
feet in sweet grass
you who used to say
I kept a fort of longing
through thistle
or is it singing
forest dark with
milk pails and marrow
black oak savannahs
became harvests

loose dress no stockings
blue jean jacket
remember
wilting summers
the other seasons
singing like it was
the aptitude
bare as undertone
always
a long time
prairie mallow
underneath my name
antiquated habits
I'm nowhere again
the leaping we did
netted winged things

Autumn Thinking

Yes, I'm talking about being a tree again.
Deciduous, thrumming with molt, I admire
sycamores shedding their golden fleets

and think, *yes, let's learn finance, chop wood,*
tattoo my arms with poppies, study entomology.
Let's tap maples, shear sheep, discover rare fungi.

It's the air, I know. It's the light.
But my autumn-other, she bites,
less mirage than maniac.

Tree, you're lucky to disperse
tiny boats of yourself, always new ones
rocking briefly in your intricate harbor.

Inept Koan

Sometimes I speak from the wounded bird.
Sometimes, grafted bone.

Sometimes I grow tired,
each day a new swimming pool.

When I speak of the husband, I draft nocturnes
to prove it was all faultless floundering.

I call out. I envy those who've kept
one job for years, who celebrate

anniversaries, raise kids, trust
their retirements to stock markets.

Who swim lap after lap after lap
without the mind's chatter chatter chatter.

All that clattering of desire and rather.
I'm no musket, no anemone.

I've tried to fit bluets into a poem
for weeks—finally. Now you see

the height of my ambition.
Now you see the wounded bird's discomfort

as it flounders from ulna to femur, each inelegant
bone another muted flute, inept koan.

Nostalgia Sweepstakes

for R.

Remember how you led me out
of the crowded party? We walked

where the ocean leaked into marsh
beneath fingers of moonlight.

In the warm boundary waters of kissing,
our bodies learned each other.

Strangers by anyone's account,
we stopped numbering

kisses, naming them instead:
hula-hoop, elevator, in the dark shed.

Long ago the stones we stacked,
one atop the other, toppled.

Memory relies on magic tricks—
green tea rescues your voice and skinny wrists—

but I almost never say your name. Even now
when it cleaves my lungs like pollen,

it never sheds its silvery skin—sweet cough,
light-fed dust, unborn flower in my chest.

Shelterbelt

for Kindra

During a bedroom photo shoot,
   you painted spirals on my breasts.
Dressed me in your leather,
   plastic gems dotting my eyes.
Your roommates certain we were dykes.

But we were wives of another kind—
   two ghosts dancing in a field,
fireflies snaking through trees faster
   than the beats spilling
from your car stereo. You twisted glow

sticks around your body—a duet, for a while,
   harbors and nightlights,
parasols and shelterbelts. In that field
   we bribed the stars to ensure
our futures shone—I think those selves

would high-five us now.
   Loss has salted us more than once—
and will again. I don't know what song
   snares you tonight. Dance with me,
distant friend, who lifts jellyfish to the moon.

Love this lad one more time.

Juneberry

Though others name you shadbush, shadblow,
saskatoon, and sugarplum, you're always June to me.
Your bruise-hued fruits fuse blueberry and apple, cherry and pear.

I planted you. Watered you, watched your orange flames
flicker in autumn, your snowy blossoms flash in spring.
You torch, fan-dancer, branches smooth as sanded glass.

On each rare visit I note your growth—I've grown, too, with less show.
You can't see new leaves sprouting on my ribs, the dangerous
flower poised beneath. I call it Hookbow.

Once you fit in my car. Now you're the size of it.
I haven't planted in years. You, the lilac, the buddleia—last
root balls I opened and bedded. If the new tenants don't praise you,

call out to me, shadbush, shadblow, sugarplum,
your blooms white and fragile as fish bones. I will prune you
to a shape like fire, name you until each leaf brightens like a kiss.

My Elizabeth

after the film, Reaching for the Moon

arrives in trousers rolled at the ankle, sunglasses
balanced on her brow, hair coiling in Brazil's hot hands,
anapests and iambics scuttling the dark
fisheries where her poems brew like eggs.

The first time she wanted a woman, she didn't skitter
like a stray dog under a kind hand; few words,
but each of them *selected.* She knows saying *passion-fruit*
ripens you, value of whispering *scrim, leap, cream.*

Maybe she doubts—surely she doubts.
But whatever hummingbird witnesses her
clap her hands twice in sudden delight
forgoes nectar, agrees to subsist on her smoky breath.

She hatches each poem one scale at a time—
gills unfolding like sunlight. Patient as weather,
she works slowly—maybe I've mistaken patience
for a bad hangover. Her laughter is an extinct species

of bird. Like the equator, you want to know
when you've crossed her. You want her gleaming,
but she's a hurricane and as fucked up as any of us.
Lick her humanness. Let her see your bruises,

her fingerprints inside them. Convince her
she's neither ghost nor alien nor giant salmon
destined to lose its necessary rivers. Even if she is,
even if when you taste her, her vanishing grits your teeth.

Key West Nature Preserve

Two pelicans plummet, crumpling
into knots of gray ink, sending sailfins
into a flurry that, if driven by joy,
would resemble a party.

The beach is no wider than my body
is long, netted with dried seaweed, rust-red.
A girl chews on the tips of her bright green hair,
phone to ear, her shoes left on the boardwalk.

Earlier, I learned a local slashed
the pelicans' bagged beaks so fish
slipped out like sand from fingers—perhaps
this girl, or the boy who arrives, embracing

her, knows the culprit. It could be them.
It could be they mend those broken birds,
volunteering at the backyard sanctuary
where the pelicans suffer silently,

their squawks sloughed after adolescence.
Stoics and clowns, elegant comics,
they skirted extinction those seasons
parents crushed their young,

eggshells thin as bad lies.
Ending DDT use is perhaps easier
than arresting a person with a knife, bored,
stuck on an island cluttered with tourists and booze,

a person certain a pelican's wound will ease
his or her own. The girl and boy enter
the mangroves. Plastic bags knot narrow trunks;
the girl coughs. I don't smell marijuana,

but I imagine it, flowering their lungs,
the girl's sadness fading like her jeans.
Pelicans plunk again into the sea. Whole,
for now: their bodies coins, luck their harvest.

First Kingdom

We claimed the pasture autumn
through spring, children turned deer-hooved
and hawk-eyed. Cattle gone for slaughter,
their kingdom of bull thistle and buckthorn
finally our own. We ate invisible meals
on stumps. Nothing stunk except sunset—
no, we still complained as children do.
Outgrew the old games like clothes.
Alone, I haunted the pasture,
fashioned a crown of teasel pods
and stickweed, horseweed and vetch,
crown vivid and disturbing
as it grew and crumbled
with each weaving. I wear it still.
The pasture's gone.
And those playmates are parents now.
Would they add nettle and speedwell
or purse their lips—*poor thing,*
divorced and childless.
I wave my queenly hand when they pass.
I add spurge and henbit.
Then I cut the ribbon, offer their children cake.

Switchgrass

Though it intimates intellectual laziness,
as well as, perhaps, perversion, I'm a little hot
for your Wikipedia entry: Rapunzel roots
twisting down dirt's castle walls
while your shock-top sucks carbon dioxide
with its hundred straws. Something chest-thumping
and cleft chin about you, gangster of the prairie.
Flexing over how many chicks you get—
by which I mean quail. By which I think
pheasant—you quarterback of grasses.
An image search piques my longing.
Gray-green and dominating, a Shaquille O'Neal
among pipsqueak grasses.
Sexhound, heartthrob, I won't lie.
There's lots of plants I'd like to fuck.
But you—tall panic grass, blackbent, thatchgrass,
you churl, you biomass energy machine—let me take you
behind the barn and show you what I mean.

Sundress in Winter

While I obsess over vanities
like *should I henna my hair,*
my uncle lies in a hospital bed,
thin as ladder rung,
fluid swallowing his lungs.
A nurse preps him for surgery.
Drains, needles, a giant straw of sorts—
                                        perhaps a funnel.

Then weeks lying around, healing.
And this kind of juxtaposition all the time.
All the time. No wonder I like to erase
myself with television.

Prayer, though I'm the worst kind of suitcase,
packed with sundresses in winter,
lead me like morning.
When I see my uncle, thin as a whisper,
turn my scarlet hair into one of your flags.

Poem for My Former Niece

Soon it will hurt less
to remember your hair
in my hands, softest foxtails.

Or your voice as you kicked
your feet in the bath.
Your five-year-old insights, zinnia-bright.

Being your aunt is winning
summer, warm rain, and
a tap-dancing unicorn.

It's chocolate cake for breakfast
and a tea party with panda bears—
please, draw that for me.

That's what I would have asked
before the divorce. Now,
in this new land, I treat you

like a unicorn. Sugar cubes
in my hand, soft whistle
in my throat.

There's no word
for "former niece."
I'd rather eat

500 pickles than invent
such a term.
I hope you laugh

about those pickles.
Rare egg, trust your shine.
Know I tend a bouquet for you.

Inventing a Seashell

after Meghan O'Rourke

Pour minerals into a fat blue jug.
Wait a long time, without looking,
without holding out your hands

for snowfall. You must read
books on geology, cosmology,
horse hooves, cauls: you must be gentle.

Sing songs of glue and bone,
gloves and lampshades; sing
of stiff bras and shoes, a winter hat.

If, after surviving a tornado, hunger,
a cold stare and complete surrender,
you learn to sail, sew a button,

gut a deer and birth a calf, you might
have the lung capacity, the eyesight
required. Walk backwards if you can.

Some would advise taking a companion;
I say you're better off alone. Wade
into thigh-deep waves, feel cold break

against your loins, reminder
you're a jar of heat and blood.
Walk into kelp's dark arms,

turn your hands into a bowl.
Then your seashell might arrive,
pure as spoon, hard as the old life.

Don't touch it.
Admire as one does a dress
or someone else's home.

Etymology of Orgasm

A riddle a burrow a furrow
cave that retreats as you arrive
cymbals grooving light
worn path yellow house
door's locked singing yellow
yellow yellow and elbow
not quite a pebble rippled
leaner kind of mean
dreamish but with more fins
climb as you collapse as you climb
this marvelous dime spinning
hey yo hey yo foxglove oh
synonym for koan give and go
pocket with a hole jazz hands
jazz hands juniper gowns
pinched and pearled eyelids off with
off with clamp that tongue mouth
on your you're wheelbarrow
jasper hound unraveling like
hey ceiling hi ceiling oh Jennifer
who's Jennifer glint hop bebop
doorstop truffle you're your oh so
oars in gravel and wow my flight path
dazzle brigade oyster-shells don't
fall oh fall hey fall up the road
up the autumn road quick tick tick
here hear it there going gone home

Saplings

Two maples sprouted in a bucket of wet ashes,
convinced me to stop looking everywhere for cancer.

One I transplanted to a field of milkweed
where it grew milky and wild as the spines of sleeping children.

The other I planted in my aunt's gutters—
when its roots scrambled through the downspout,

we knew the foundation was secure.
It's not a world of termites in the end.

Not a world of hornets nesting in an empty birdfeeder.
Because I saw three honeybees pulling nectar

from joe-pye weed, I trusted my parents and brothers
would wake up another day, eat cereal, trim their toenails.

Then wind picked up the pink sprays of buddleia,
bleached whiskers of maiden grass, and I knew

I was lost to a feeling shaped like a hula-hoop.
Call it giddiness. Call it tightrope. But I swore

I'd never complain again, never worry about what wasn't.

Pearly Everlasting

Someone gave the name, sometime, of pearly everlasting
to those white buttons joined to stems with yellow thread,
prairie flirts I dry from hooks above the sink.

Coffee in chipped mugs, pancakes stuffed with blueberries
plucked from bushes we planted years ago—later you'll mow
the lawn and I'll weed the garden. Time for poems

and reading in the sun—endless, here, and all our family
and friends live within a mile. We walk after dinner,
then back home under starlight, listening for coyotes.

In winter: fires. In spring: new chickens.
Once you bound yourself in dozens of ribbons
for me to open you one by one. Once, you licked

warm honey from our hives off my stomach.
It's moonlight and molasses all the time
even when it isn't. This is the life I pretend you've invented

for us. Maybe you'd include mountains where I'd put meadow.
A fool's dream. Sorrow and its gang have other plans—
the kind that, despite bad weather and poor communication,

never fall through. Love, the imagined world
is a ruin of the real one. Love, remember how we saw
a pair of red foxes across the creek?

They dipped their dark noses into cold water.
They bent to thirst and what thirst offers.

Notes

"Charlottesville, 7 a.m." borrows the line "winter lives under a pigeon's wing,"
from Elizabeth Bishop's poem "Paris, 7am."

~

The first line of "Pearly Everlasting" is the last line in Robert Hass's book *Sun Under Wood*, and its foxes are the book's first images.

~

"Shelterbelt" owes a debt of gratitude to "My Amaryllis" by Deborah Digges.

Acknowledgments

Thank you to the following publications, which published these poems, sometimes by different titles and in different forms:

Adroit Literary Journal: "The Unknotting"
Baltimore Review: "Spell for the End of Grief" and "Rattlesnake Master"
Coal Hill Review: "Dream of the Ark"
Copper Nickel: "Saplings"
Dorothy Sargent Rosenberg Poetry Prize: "Drowning the Marigold" and
    "Nostalgia Sweepstakes"
Gettysburg Review: "Ten Walls"
Louisiana Cultural Vistas: "Blackberry Season" and "Velleity"
North American Review: "Last Visit"
Passages North: "Hayloft" and "The White Doe"
Smartish Pace: "First Visitation"
The Missouri Review, Poem of the Week: "Autumn Thinking"
Yemassee: "Crush"

~

Thank you to Ava Leavell Haymon for selecting "Blackberry Season" and
"Velleity" for the Tennessee Williams/New Orleans Literary Festival 2012
Poetry Prize. Thank you to *Smartish Pace* for selecting "First Visitation" as
the winner of the 2013 Beullah Rose Prize. Thank you to the Dorothy Sargent
Rosenberg Poetry Prize for selecting "Drowning the Marigold" and "Nostalgia
Sweepstakes" for recognition in 2013. Buckets of gratitude to the Vermont
Studio Center and the Key West Literary Seminar for the time and space to
compose and revise these poems.

Heartfelt and bone-deep thanks to my parents, Mark and Cheryl Whittemore,
for their unequivocal support. This book is dedicated to my entire family, but
particularly to the memory of my grandparents, Bob and Bea Whittemore.

And, to my teachers, more thanks than I could ever adequately bestow—

thank you Brigit Pegeen Kelly, Beth Lordan, Rodney Jones, Judy Jordan, and Allison Joseph.

Thank you to my readers, for their insights, edits, and unflappable support: Jenna Bazzell, Ed Brunner, Sarah McCartt-Jackson, Andrew McFayden-Ketchum, Travis Mossotti, Hannah New, and all of my fellow writers at Southern Illinois University Carbondale's MFA program. Thank you to my writing group for your intelligent criticism and unwavering faith: Patricia Asuncion, Stephanie Bernhard, Carly Griffith, Elizabeth Klaczynski, Laura Kolbe, and Rebecca Taylor. Thank you to my editor, Christine Stroud, and everyone at Autumn House Press for their faith in my work.

~

Finally and always, thank you to Tim Shea.

The Autumn House Poetry Series

• Winner of the annual Autumn House Poetry Prize

* *Coal Hill Review* chapbook series